BEND OF QUIET

Kenneth Pobo

I0203386

BLUE LIGHT PRESS ❖ 1ST WORLD PUBLISHING

1ST WORLD PUBLISHING

SAN FRANCISCO ❖ FAIRFIELD ❖ DELHI

WINNER OF THE 2014 BLUE LIGHT BOOK AWARD

BEND OF QUIET

Copyright ©2015 by Kenneth Pobo

All rights reserved. Printed in the United States of America. No part of this book may be used or reproduced in any manner whatsoever without written permission except in the case of brief quotations embodied in critical articles and reviews. For information contact:

1ST WORLD LIBRARY
PO Box 2211
Fairfield, IA 52556
www.1stworldpublishing.com

BLUE LIGHT PRESS
www.bluelightpress.com
Email: bluelightpress@aol.com

BOOK & COVER DESIGN
Melanie Gendron

COVER ART
"Birds at the Feeder" by Melanie Gendron

AUTHOR PHOTO
Stan Slater

FIRST EDITION

Library of Congress Control Number: 2015950590

ISBN 9781421837413

BEND OF QUIET

TABLE OF CONTENTS

1. Open Cages

2. Varieties

FOR STAN

ACKNOWLEDGMENT

I would like to thank the editors of these magazines for publishing work from this collection:

"Wet Eyes" *Poetry Down Under*
"Polar Bear at the Zoo" *Skylark*
"Panda Passing" Forpoetry.com, *And We the Creatures* (anthology), Dream Horse Press
"Hibernation" *Wascana Review*
"Harp Seal" Forpoetry.com
"Boat Ride" *Verse Wisconsin*
"Minnows under the Boat" *Midwest Quarterly*
"I Row Closer" originally published as "Turtles on a Log" *Thema*
"Bask" *Bluff City*
"Dog" *Iodine*
"Spine" *El Gato Tuerto*
"Spider in the Drain" *Midwest Quarterly*
"Rat Rap" *Native West Press*
"Scorpion Sex and Death" *Abbey*
"Worker Bee" *Mobius*
"Cicada Promise" *Grain*
"Grasshopper" *Epicenter*
"Mantis" *Facets*
"Mosquito Blizzard" *Gival Press*
"Sticks" *Thorny Locust*
"Pigeons" *Mudfish*
"Finch Friends" *Miller's Pond Review*
"Bird Feeder" *American Tanka*
"Just Now" *Hibiscus*

"Common Ground" *Mobius*
"Varieties" *Buckle &*
"Wang Wei Says" *DuPage Valley Review*
"Pink Ladyslippers" *Red Owl*
"Cosmos" *Links*
"Attacking a Boxwood" *Autumn Sky*
"Tree Sparks" *Urbanus*
"Elegy for a Limb" *The Darfur Anthology*
"Impossible Lover" *Apple Valley Review*
"Dumb Birds" *Welter*
"Glads" *Acta Victoriana*
"Storm" *West Branch*
"Lawn Dreams" *Slant*
"Back Yard Birch" *Message in a Bottle*; *The Organic Writer*
"Persephone And Pomegranates" *Fruita Pulp*
"Late Summer Nursery" *Moonshot*
"Praise for Tall Asters" *Picayune Magazine*
"Stones" *Buddhist Poetry Review*
"November Bouquet" *One Trick Pony*
"Winter-ruption" *Wild Goose Poetry Review*
"Winter Fig" *Centrifugal Eye*
"Crocustoms" *Wild Goose Poetry Review*
"Seedlings Before a Cold Snap" *Lightning Bell*
"Early Red Quince" *Northern Cardinal Review*
"Bend of Quiet" *The Blue Fifth*
"Accepting Brevity" *Pea River Journal*

I.

OPEN CAGES

WET EYES

At night the zookeeper
heads home past a maze
of malls, unlocks her own

cage door, lets herself in,
lets herself out, eats,
mates, returns to the zoo

in the morning, hears a hiss
and howl, ducks a
claw swipe.

An eight-foot cobra curls
up under a light bulb. Bears
scrape marshmallow off coats.

Rain today. Each drop,
another pair of wet eyes
driven deep into fur.

POLAR BEAR AT THE ZOO

On his back legs,
nose up, he stands
as if in a ballet. Does he

think of Arctic nights as we
toss popcorn and peanuts?
Do flashbulbs pop him

back to northern lights
swirling over jagged
ice islands? He turns

his back to us. We head
for apes. Others take
our place. He's still dancing

as snowbirds take off
in the tundra of his eyes,
midnight sun on paw pads.

PANDA PASSING

She's going, her panda
spirit finally returning
to China. No legal trap
can hold her--the body

is what she leaps out of.
The zoo looks strange.
Now she can roam where
her ancestors roamed
before missionaries
and guns came. People

cry over empty spaces
where cameras have
nothing to aim for. She
can't hear us.

A river swings
into view. Grass. Small
indigo flowers around
her paws. As wind
meets her fur, she
climbs a rusty hill,

the sun, gold straw
in an owl's nest.

HIBERNATION

If I could sleep
through a season, I'd rejoice —

except I wouldn't wait out
winter. I'd quit summer
when cars clutter roads
and mowers behead dandelions.
I'd miss my snowfire

rose's rap, but I could dream
of red blossoms with a white
fire center, dream

that I'm a grizzly, wandering
in a world that never stops
opening.

HARP SEAL

She takes whiteness
of snow for a skin,

the Arctic a ringing bell
she can hear even
through wind. When
humans come close, she
stays still. We want

her pelt — ice doesn't
drift quickly enough
to help her. Our hands
aren't the only terror devices:
the Arctic wastes away. On

warmer currents, oils and poisons
float up to her black nose,
black eyes — her frozen world

slips farther off. She too
retreats, shadow on snow,
her home cracking.

BOAT RIDE

On Little Lake St. Germain, an eagle
shadows our rowboat. Over a couple
of decades ago, DDT thinned their
eggs. The eagle and osprey became rare.
When the poisoning ended, they returned,
so the lake looks more as it did when I
chased minnows.
            I'd like to think that we've learned
how even the strongest can quickly die.

I picture polar bears, weakening ice
under their paws. Animals pay the price
for our greed. I try to enjoy two loons
diving and rising, diving and rising,
but it's no use. The Earth gets terrible wounds.
Our nightmare hands can strangle anything.

MINNOWS UNDER THE BOAT

I row through lily pads
to a reedy sandbar,
a tongue sticking out.

Minnows zigzag,
dart off quickly,
like an owl's hoot.

When I lie in a rented bed,
the moon thumbing me
like magazine pages.

I ROW CLOSER

to the log. Too close,
turtles leap under waves

so I row out. One by one,
they return. The lake,

a waiting room, lily
pads on the ceiling.

BASK

Redwing blackbirds
toss morning away.

Four green heads
on a wet branch
floating in open
water lilies.

Each shell,
a map,
a family tree.

Don't disturb them.
Row around the bend,
drop anchor,

bask.

DOG

98 degrees on a July day.
Sun shoots yellow bullets at every lawn.
Chained tight, the neighbor's dog can't get away,
while they sit in air-conditioning, stay
comfortable, doors closed, shades drawn.

Sometimes the German Shepherd bays,
no playmates or chasing games. She can't
find shade to get out of heat's way.
Pacing, her water dish empty,
food gone.

Weather forecasters say the same for tomorrow.
She's left out 24 hours — dusk and dawn,
like a fly, a squirrel or a bluejay.
98 degrees on a July day.
Chained tight, the neighbor's dog can't get away.

SPINE

Two things both bend
and give hope:
a weeping willow
a cat's back.

My cat, an acrobat
in his spine,
bends so many ways,
leaps, flops.
Pure jelly, his bones
sink beneath my fingers.

A cat is furry quicksand.

No cat loves
geometry — they have
no straight lines,
only bends,
as willows have bends.

RATTLER REBUTTAL

Writhe
rattle and
roll: what
I do. Sure,
my poison
kills. You're human.
Yours kills
as effectively.

When scared
I rattle.
You quiver.
Are we so
different?

You overturn rocks,
spy on fields,
poke your always
open eyes
into any
hiding place.

You eat
or bag me
for churches:
tossing me
proves faith.
I twist
away, bite
when I know
death is my handler.

SPIDER IN THE DRAIN

I postpone bathing to study
his green-ribbed back,
demanding leg scrawls.

This must be the moon
to him, a white surface.
He camps out and dreams
of stronger webs, flies
who deliver themselves
to his perfect strands.

Friends say he should
bring up revulsion;
he is, after all,
grotesque. He sits
as if he could build
a cupboard
out of his need —

I must lend him my privacy.

RAT RAP

Rats carry themselves
with dignity, panache, sneak
into impossible places.

Our saints strain
toward impossible places,
especially heaven.
Even with prayer,
we're pretty clumsy.

Not so the rat
who darts and slips
in effortlessly. We revile them
for making a home from trash,
feasting on decay.

In Vegas I saw rats
behind a big casino, hungry
on the move. Inside
the casino, people
gnawed themselves
before slots and tables.

Like rats, they
were also trapped.

SCORPION SEX AND DEATH

His pedipalps catch hers.
Under a strobe moon
they dance, do it,

part. Babies take
eighteen months. After
birth they climb up
on her bus back
for two weeks, crave
nights, gobble spiders,
sometimes each other.

On a desert, a scorpion
country singer walks out
of an empty honky tonk,
enters darkness. An owl
sees something move,
drops —

a hadrurus scorpion
on this, his last night.

Red cactus blossoms
closed tight
give no warning —
the owl, ready,
talons out.

WORKER BEE

When I carry
the sun on my wings,
I tell it about salmon
snapdragon chambers.
A sunflower bursts
open by a gutter.
Roomy and dense,
time a yellow blossom
I crawl around. Late
September, a whiff
of my own death.

CICADA PROMISE

We waited for something to break,
a July storm.

Their coming brought darkness.
Sitting outdoors scared us:
Ya never know when one'll land on ya.
It was, briefly, beautiful not knowing.
Wings, trees, sidewalks littered with green
husks, sleepless nights when they
called and sang.

Our neighbor, Mrs. Gustafson, said
cicadas have magic powers,
saw magic in root
beer bubbles, in lighting an oven.

Cicadas flittered down gutters,
hung on clotheslines,
then dropped to a lengthy sleep.

Another seventeen years
would pass before our trees
became their harps. Would they return
to a world almost undiscovered —
each founding some new America,
a yard vast in green promise?

Who would be here then?

GRASSHOPPER

You jump twenty times
your body length
with six legs. If I
could do that I'd sell my Ford,
leap from the shed's wobbly wall
to a yucca's sharpening straps.

How would I act at work
if I could spit that brown junk
you spit when riled — slime exclaims
better than a dirty look.

And five eyes! Peripheral
of peripheral vision.

Yet all's not gold in hopperland.
Flies eat your eggs, embed
their own eggs on you.
Hatched flies devour you.
A birth bed is a dinner table.

Ants cart your hind femoras off,
lithe legs lost in tall,
quiet grass.

MANTIS

In a buttercup's
laboratory,
a bee's
a traffic light
turns green.
I stop to trap him
with my eyes. He
doesn't look
like he's praying.
For what would
he pray? Sun?
He's got bales of it.
I walk toward a bell
heather, bees
exploring lavender
eggs, spiraling
up toward the gutter,
going off
while the mantis
stays still,
stays
still.

MOSQUITO BLIZZARD

Snow again! Icicles build
clear hives from gutters. I

pour tea, remember Wisconsin's
June woods, how I slapped,

cursed mosquitoes, my pleasure
in ferns and mulleins

lost. Today each flake lands,
bites, keeps me inside:

winter's way
of making mosquitoes.

MEETING AN OLD FRIEND
for Katie Andraski

A quarter
of a century since we last met,
"How are you?" so flimsy.

She tells me about the horses
on her farm, the shock
of seeing whooping cranes
after sweeping out stalls.
I've never seen a single whooper,
but have seen a

water
lily
just inches below
a heron
flying in
to shore.

Years
between us
take wing.

STICKS

The male great blue heron
brings her a stick. No heat
till she accepts.

Early on, we had many rituals,
talked on the phone for hours
about music, argued over
songs. Sometimes you'd get
so inside yourself, I couldn't
get a shovel sharp enough
to cut through stone.

Herons do the stick schtick,
decide quick. Eleven years,
we refuse, accept each other's
sticks. Yet our nest

keeps getting built.

PIGEONS

Pigeons bump along,
rafter by rafter,
crumb by crumb,
a city under wings.
Yellow taxis, beaks
between lamps. Up —

slate-colored feathers,
dirty socks.
Father O'Healy slips on
peanut shells and bits
of meat. They coo him
into church, a rosary
around his neck
fibrillating. Pigeons

leave few tracks,
but you see them everywhere,
eyes darting left and right,
wide open.

FINCH FRIENDS

We hang the stocking-like feeder
from the maple's lowest arm.
Three finches follow the leader
once we're gone. Door closed,
in our dining room, we watch them joy
around, flit, fly and return.

Pinwheel sunrays turn in leaves. A toy
sky breaks into pieces of cloud.
Finch yellow — brighter than fabrics
we dye and sew, much more stylish.
New arrivers keep coming,

push July onto grass, grab a brief
space to eat from an elongated dish.

BIRD FEEDER

Bird feeder, you call
and call. It's not even long
distance. If only one
chickadee would answer! If
only the squirrels wouldn't.

JUST NOW

a bluebird
flies out
of an icicle,
drops feathers
in mud, dis-
appears
in thin trees,
aims for the sun —
long winter,
her whistle
no call
to come follow,
only silence
bending.

2.
VARIETIES

COMMON GROUND

Ground isn't common —

it cradles asters, zinnias,
Jacob's Ladders, larkspurs
and roses, provides a home,
a good education from the sky,

doesn't try to turn an anemone
into a strawflower.

Ground says, "The Party's Here!"

Flowers stir a bright color
cauldron, dance.

VARIETIES

My five Jacob's Ladders,
as different

as anyone's children,
perhaps more so. Some

blue, some pink, and
the dwarf's got greenish

brown trumpets. Asters,
countries which require

no passport, no security check.
Bees lead. We follow.

Pie-plate and pompom dahlias,
meadow rue, our

human garden,
much the same, yet

we exterminate
varieties we don't like.

WANG WEI SAYS

he just ambled down
a mountain where he saw

a trillium — honest,
he says, leaves half hid it,

but when I bent
to look closely, the center

held twelve numerals
from a clock that leapt

into it and died,
free of time at last.

PINK LADYSLIPPERS!

We put-put out to an
empty island. Since when
is a place with oaks
and pines empty?

Dad used to take me
to the island,
a Blatz Beer sign
on the resort beach
a quarter mile away.
Just as we're ready
to leave, can it be?
four pink ladyslippers.

Intruders lugging bait
and beer cans, we toss
them a last glance,
slop back in the boat,
slide through
urgent
yellow
water lilies.

COSMOS

She spent most of the summer
building a lace Parthenon.
Buds, statues that children built

from earth and sand, sun
rising in the eyes of
a single raindrop,

came to life late in August,
before winter turned them
into conquered land:

lavender scraped off by white
ice blossoms,
statues fled.

ATTACKING A BOXWOOD

It has seen maybe thirty years
of storms and gooseberries
by a climbing rose. We plot

death, want the space it sprawls on
for flowers. I cut crazily
for a good half hour
till it's barely a stump.
But not dead.

You rev the chain saw —
even the stump must go.

Branches, how green they are.
Shining.

Our shirts smell of death.
Partners in life
and now in a killing,

we drop boxwood pieces
into the compost heap,
sneak in the back door.

DISMANTLING A CACTUS

This prickly pear sprawls too much,
all for three blossoms a year.
I decide to dismantle it —

without gloves. Pad by pad
I pull and twist, needles piercing
hand and arm. Green flip-flops

on grass. Gaining room,
an Oso Paprika Rose
will fame into flower —

no cactus cups this year,
Athena returning my invitations,
miffed that I'd dismantle heaven.

TREE SPARKS

Fire shooting off
    your branches
    makes even me
    like summer.
How rotten can a season
    be if yellow
                 flowers

    upend the tidy diligence
    of a backyard tree?

    Tree of Arson,
        you turn us
    into burning roofs.

ELEGY FOR A LIMB

On wet ground, a dead maple limb
I had meant to saw off for
months. A storm has taken him.
He looks stronger than before.
I slip on grass as I carry
him to the side of the house. He
takes my saw's bite with no
groan. I cut him into
segments. A hole, black as a crow,
shows how deep his wound went.
Bark hid his decline. Rot grew
quietly, gave no scent.
Trashmen will clatter on Monday —
toss him in, carry him away.

IMPOSSIBLE LOVER

Each day you give your garden
more love than you give to people.

He makes demands —
you feed him, spend a fortune
trying to please him. He only laughs,
infects you with Lyme disease and poison ivy.
Sun or rain, he snaps his fingers. You come

quickly. He doesn't desire just you,
lets in deer, groundhogs, Japanese beetles.
Your adoration won't stop
his promiscuous invitations. Often
in the kitchen, you say to yourself,

"Not today. He can wilt in the heat
for all I care." Five minutes later
you're out, carrying him a drink.

DUMB BIRDS

Ask my neighbor Lenny
his favorite TV show and he says
"*Mannix*. There hasn't been
a good show since then."
As for animals, he prefers them all
extinct, especially pets.
"They mess up the yard. Birds
are the worst. What's dumber
than a bird?"

Lenny is like a suitcase
with nothing in it.

I think of telling him
about my great conversation
with a cardinal yesterday,
a learned cardinal,
not one to be imprecise.

The flashing red wings . . .

Bah, Lenny would say —
and then go inside
to watch the Weather Channel
tell him the weather
every 8 minutes
every 8 minutes
every 8 minutes.

WHITMAN WEEDING

My garden contains multitudes
of weeds. Actually,

I don't have a garden, am too
crippled to pull creeping

charley. My flowers open
between syllables, are more

vast than my mind. Some call me
puffed up. My ex-boss

called my leaves dirty and
fired me. Perhaps he knew little

of autumn. Trees don't keep
leaves spotless, like dishes

my mother washed. Rain,
mud and leaves, the eternal trio.

I watch my neighbor pull
dandelions. Their roots pay

the same rent as roses. My dream
garden, a brambly beard,

a hotel full of songbirds
singing all day, all night.

GLADIOLAS

Some call gladiolas
old-fashioned — flowers
grandmothers prefer,

farm women with
husbands in fields,
gladiolas gaping in
a spunky garden.
Mine aren't quaint —
they're punk,
in your face,
they disturb and coax.

Reds and purples bunch,
sunsets on stalks, painted
wicker chairs
or a boar's
bloody tooth.

STORM

These silences —

as a child, sky
the color of my bruised thigh:
elms shaking without sound.

Sometimes I walk
in the cemetery.
It's quiet there —
buds, pink and deepening
along tree limbs, red
against stone. Alone,
I read a stranger's name,
catching my own
reflection in a pool.

Now winds surge. Big drops
slide down my face.
Rain grows heavier,
an early memory, some chill
trying to get inside me,
my name trying to get free.

LAWN DREAMS

Light's not baking bread
in an oak's oven.
No squirrels
in any leafy kitchen
No electricity,
just moon mica
falling on asters.

Dawn lights the stove.
Branches, huge spoons,
stir clouds. The lawn
tells my window her dreams.

BACK YARD BIRCH

Tall Wisconsin birches
line the highway. Light sifts
down, leaves almost translucent.
If I were the moon, I'd talk
all night with a birch. I'm just
a guy with too much weeding to do.

One birch provides good conversation.
Small, airy, a tree with nothing
to prove. I put violas
at its base, an offering.

Catbirds sing in undergrowth,
the birch a fine launching spot
on their way to a blueberry bush.
Tails high, wrens duet,
brown against birch white.

A gray winter sky wraps
empty branches. Spring
will come. Watched by the blue
eyes of forget-me-nots,
the birch will be ready.

PERSEPHONE AND POMEGRANATES

Budding in full sun, our pomegranate tree
forgets the trouble it caused thousands
of years ago. Persephone wanted to escape.

She missed the tart odor of a meadow,
the cold quiet of an autumn apple orchard.
She got a yen for pomegranates,
sucking the fruit dry, eating the seeds,
freedom a stroll away. Demeter had arranged

for Earth to be blooming, pomegranate
trees fruiting. Persephone returned but
had to go back to the blowhard
who knew her weakness for red juice

on her lips. Demeter savaged
the Earth's ripeness, waited for those seasons
when she and her daughter would walk together,
eating pomegranates, faces stained
in a drowsy dusk.

LATE SUMMER NURSERY

September shrinks like wax paper
before a lit match. Aisles of petunias,
gone. Lilies trashed or hidden.

Some flowers still perform — red-shoed
dahlias, Japanese anemones
like budding antennae. Mums,
ready to break
into autumn's house.

Back in July I'd dodge bees
as I swerved between pots and plots.
A few linger, late customers. I think
of spring bulbs not quite ready for sale.
And Christmas, such nervous joy.

PRAISE FOR TALL ASTERS

Such a chilly day and gray.
This Syracuse, New York, winter
sky has come for a long visit
to southern Pennsylvania. I wish

the sun would risk an icy walk.
I'll set the table. We could roast weenies.

Outside the window, something wonderful . . .

     Asters,
     lavender petaled
     with yellow centers,
     fully open.

The gray may stretch for miles,
no match for these asters
who don't seem to notice.

STONES

Kindness is a stone
under the shock
of red on cardinal
flowers.

Unkindness is a stone
thrown hard, the shock
of wounds
that never heal.

A stone takes sun
and moon. Night climbs up
on its shoulders,
sees dawn being born.

NOVEMBER BOUQUET

I've got no grouse with November,
welcome it after long sweaty days,
carry my scissors to whatever remains
in bloom: asters, mums, toad lilies,
and a deep red Mirandy rose. My hands
fill with flowers, possibilities,

love. A cold snap will surely
blacken them. I have a vase ready,
cobalt blue against window sun,
and blossoms that don't believe
in winter, or if they do, they open,

they deepen in color,
ignoring the wind's gossip.

WINTER-RUPTION

Daffodil and aconite bulbs crave
cold's touch under frozen mud.
While we hang pictures we meant to hang
for months, cover ourselves in

blue afghans, wind makes awnings
sound like off-kilter washing machines —
the first snowflake drops,
a white rock on a leaf's torn back.

WINTER FIG

We burlap it in winter, can't
keep out crowbars of wind.
Deer chomp and bound
past catalpa trees.

Some cold days, it shivers,
roots in a clay soil bowl.
Fruit. A promise
that maybe can't be kept.

CROCUSTOMS

Under wet brown leaves,
crocuses break

purple cups of buds,
climb a dirt stairway
to find sun, bask
a couple of weeks.
They open as tomorrow
turns his back on them.

With only a few hours
to count on,
they shimmer.

SEEDLINGS FACING A COLD SNAP

Each year I start them
too soon — hyacinth beans
twine into artificial lights.

Leggy calendulas, thin
trunks hardly able to hoist
two leaves. Spring loiters,

won't be forced like paperwhites.
I put them out, fear
tomorrow night's cold

will bring frost,
the Angel of Death
passing over, only this Angel

often drops in.
While I pull up covers,
seedling roots recoil

from ice hands. Dawn
reveals the dead
and doomed.

EARLY RED QUINCE

The quince stares December down.
Barely hidden behind pines,
thief January steals color.

The quince waves a red flag.
One frozen night it will turn
white, surrender —

an empty place where
no fruit will form.

BEND OF QUIET

In the morning, a scorcher ahead,
Stan still asleep, the cats play
hockey with pens and 45 spindles.

I'd better water. The hose lacks
a snake's stealth and surprise.
Spray covers impatiens. Heat

wraps sunflowers, yet they
stand fierce. In this bend of quiet,

no cars, the road already too warm
for bare feet. A coral tigridia
unveils her spots. A pink
and white hibiscus drops pollen

between a culver's root's
white spires.

ACCEPTING BREVITY

The epiphyllum blooms,
two days at most.

A coral thread
sews the world together.

ABOUT THE AUTHOR

Kenneth Pobo has five books and twenty chapbooks published. His work has appeared in: *Hawaii Review, Antigonish Review, Nimrod, Mudfish, Indiana Review, Weber: The Contemporary West,* and elsewhere. He began writing poetry in 1970. He teaches creative writing and English at Widener University in Pennsylvania.

Printed in the United States of America

www.ingramcontent.com/pod-product-compliance
Lightning Source LLC
Chambersburg PA
CBHW022040090426
42741CB00007B/1145